The First Thanksgiving Feast

BY JOAN ANDERSON

PHOTOGRAPHED BY
GEORGE ANCONA

CLARION BOOKS

TICKNOR & FIELDS : A HOUGHTON MIFFLIN COMPANY

NEW YORK

To Dr. Jay Anderson/J. A.

To Margarida, *comadre*/G. A.

We would like to thank the staff of Plimoth Plantation for opening up their doors to enable us to depict the historically accurate re-creation of the first Thanksgiving feast. We're especially grateful to Rosemary Carroll for all her help in coordinating the project with such good humor and friendship. We're indebted to Richard Ehrlich for his encouragement and to James Baker for his invaluable historical expertise. We are also thankful to Daisy Moore, Tony Pollard, Gkisedtanamoogk, and the other Wampanoag interpreters for their participation and the contribution of their perspective as Native People.

Especially, we would like to thank Paul Cripps, Len Travers, and the other Pilgrim interpreters who brought to life the rugged characters of our fore-fathers, giving the book a 17th-century reality.

Special thanks to Anita Joeckel, children's librarian, for encouraging this project.

Finally, our gratefulness to Mr. and Mrs. J. Allan Anderson for their hospi-tality and good fellowship after the long days' work.

Joan Anderson and George Ancona

Clarion Books/Ticknor & Fields, a Houghton Mifflin Company
Text copyright © 1984 by Joan Anderson/Photographs copyright © 1984 by George Ancona

Library of Congress Cataloging in Publication Data
Anderson, Joan.
  The first Thanksgiving feast.
  Summary: Re-creates the first harvest feast celebrated by the Pilgrims in 1621 using the Pilgrim and Indian actors and the seventeenth-century setting of Plimoth Plantation, a living history museum in Plymouth, Massachusetts.
  1. Massachusetts—History—New Plymouth, 1620-1691—Juvenile literature. 2. Pilgrims (New Plymouth colony)—Juvenile literature. 3. Thanksgiving Day—Juvenile literature.
[1. Massachusetts—History—New Plymouth, 1620-1691. 2. Pilgrims (New Plymouth colony) 3. Thanksgiving Day] I. Ancona, George, ill. II. Title.
F68.A54 1984   974.4′02   84-5804
ISBN 0-89919-287-4 PA ISBN 0-395-51886-5

H   10 9 8 7 6

*I*n September of 1620, a sturdy ship called the *Mayflower* left Plymouth, England, with 102 passengers aboard. Half of these men, women, and children were Separatists, so-called because they had broken away from the national Church of England to worship in their own way. The others were members of the Church of England who were looking for greater economic opportunity in the New World.

In November, the *Mayflower* arrived at Cape Cod in New England. The passengers, later known as the Pilgrims, decided to establish a permanent home there. The Separatists called themselves "saints" and referred to the others as "strangers." Despite their differences, the saints and strangers began a small settlement in December at a place called "the thievish harbor," or Plymouth. They named their new home Plymouth Plantation.

During the first winter and spring, half the original settlers died. But the survivors, with the help of their Indian neighbors, managed to plant crops and to reap a good harvest. They wanted to celebrate.

The First Thanksgiving Feast re-creates this first harvest festival. It was photographed at Plimoth Plantation, a living history museum of 17th-century life in Plymouth, Massachusetts. The museum uses an alternate spelling of Plymouth to distinguish it from the town itself. The people at Plimoth Plantation, called interpreters, live and speak just as the Pilgrims did. The Indians are Wampanoags, descendants of the Native People who were in large part responsible for the survival of the Plymouth colony. The dialogue is fictional. It is based on the first-hand accounts of the original feast found in the books *Of Plymouth Plantation* and *Mourt's Relation*.

*T*he days were getting shorter. Cape Cod Bay was sending cool, crisp breezes into the tiny new village of Plymouth that lay upon its shore. The year was 1621, and the Pilgrims had just gathered in their first harvest.

Governor William Bradford and his assistants, Edward Winslow and Stephen Hopkins, were meeting to discuss village matters.

Over a year had passed since these Pilgrims had sailed away from their homeland. They were proud Englishmen, living now in the wilderness of New England.

    " 'Tis harvest time in England now," Edward Winslow said. "The farmers there will have stored all their crops. Soon the Harvest Home festival will begin."

    "Yes, indeed," said Stephen Hopkins. "Would it not be a fine idea to have a merry festival here as well?"

    Governor Bradford listened to his Assistant Governors, but he was always mindful of God first. "The Lord has been good to us. Do you not think we should have a day of prayer and thanksgiving instead?"

    "You mean a day of giving thanks

instead of a festival?" both Winslow and Hopkins asked at the same time.

"Perhaps," the Governor said.

"Oh, no, sir," Hopkins replied hastily. "Winslow and I do favor a feast. We spend no time making merry. Feasting and recreation would be good for our village spirit."

Governor Bradford thought silently for a moment. "Yes," he agreed, "our villagers have reason enough for a joyous celebration. Now that we have gathered a good harvest, we feel more confident that we can survive in this new land."

SUSANNAH WINSLOW
wife of Edward Winslow
mother of two
saint

" 'Twas not so pleasant spending sixty-
six days aboard that tiny ship, the
Mayflower. We never knew if we
would reach our destination. 'Twas
most comforting that God gave us
once again the sight of land. How
grateful we were when we set foot
on solid ground."

ISAAC ALLERTON
widower
father of two
saint

"I had hoped that the *Mayflower* would take us farther south. But due to tides and currents and the lateness of the year, we found ourselves here. I was most fearful because of tales about the ill feelings the Indians did have for the white man. This 'thievish harbor' was said to be heavily populated with Indians. But I and the other members of our search party found no one to fear."

JOHN ALDEN
unmarried
stranger

"I was in the search party that stumbled upon a hill of sand under which was a great basket. It was full to the brim with fair kernels of Indian corn. After giving the matter prayerful consideration, we filled a kettle with the kernels and took it aboard the *Mayflower.* We thought we would pay the Indians for their corn when at last we met up with them."

PETER BROWNE
unmarried
stranger

"Thanks be to God that we found
fields already cleared for planting.
Imagine the hours of labor it would
have taken to cut down trees, pull out
stumps, and carry away rocks. We
would not have been able to plant a
single seed until late summer, and
that would have done us hardly any
good. Cleared fields assured us of
a goodly harvest."

GEORGE SOULE
widower
stranger

"God be praised that we had strength to build seven houses in a very short time. Despite rain and cold and sickness, we did hammer and saw and thatch. 'Twas a fine decision that each man build his own house. That way, men worked more hastily than if they helped their fellow villagers as well."

ELIZABETH HOPKINS
wife of Stephen Hopkins
mother of four
stranger

"Praise God, my family is alive and did survive 'the general sickness.' When my dear husband fell ill, along with three or four others a day, I almost gave up all hope. Some days, there were but one or two to care for the others in their retching and fever and, yes, even death. But God in his infinite love took only half our people. He left the rest of us as instruments for his work in this 'new' England."

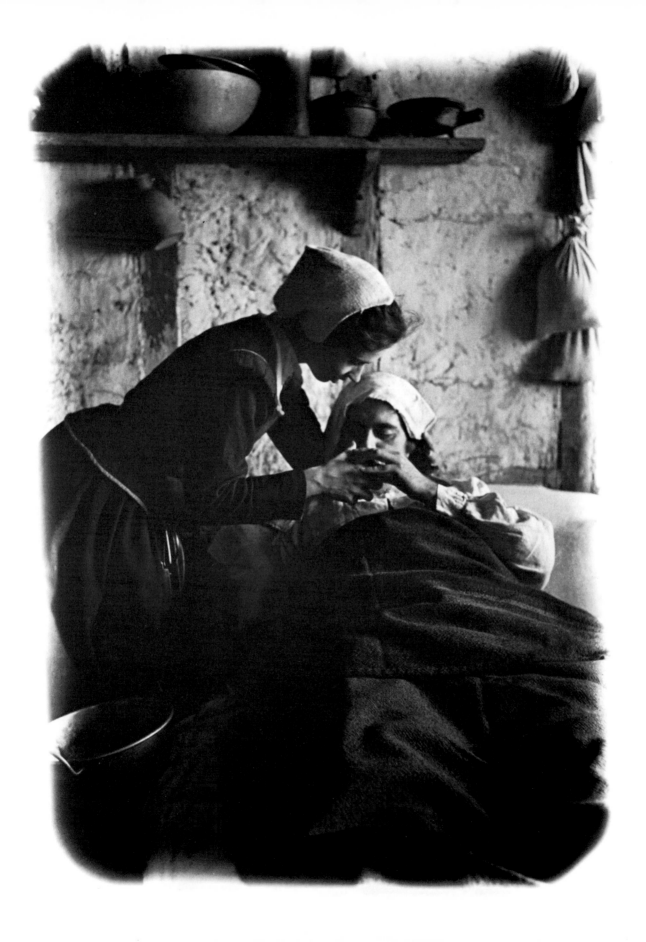

MYLES STANDISH
unmarried
stranger

"I will never forget that cold March
day when the Indian named Samoset
suddenly appeared in our street. We
were taken by surprise, and I had not
time to even grab my musket. But
he greeted us with 'Welcome, welcome, Englishmen.' We invited him to
stay the night, and we finally learned
why there were cleared, unclaimed
fields. The Indians who did live here
had died in a plague, which left our
Plymouth area empty. Our fear of
Indians did diminish that very night."

MARY BREWSTER
wife of William Brewster
mother of two
saint

"I was most joyous to meet Samoset's friend Squanto, who in April did give us a lesson in planting corn. Good thing, too, because our English pease and wheat did not grow well in the hot sunshine. First, Squanto dug a hole, into which he placed two or three herring to give food to the soil. Then he filled in the hole, placed four kernels of corn on top, and formed a little hill of soil over them. Now we have a wonderful corn harvest, enough that each person will have a peck of meal a week."

GOVERNOR BRADFORD
widower
saint

"Praise be to God that we made a treaty of peace with the Indians. 'Twas only a few days after Samoset's visit that he brought back Squanto and Massasoit, chief of the great Wampanoag nation. How good that after some talk and socializing with the Indians, John Carver, our first Governor, did put quill to paper and sign an agreement of amity and good faith. Massasoit's nation does control many tribes beyond our plantation. Now Plymouth can feel safe living with these neighboring people."

ELEANOR BILLINGTON
wife of John Billington
mother of two
stranger

"I do rejoice in having fellowship with our Indian neighbors. We have learned so many important things from them. They are very trusty and ripe-witted."

RICHARD WARREN
husband of Elizabeth Warren
father of five
stranger

"We want for nothing. We have much cod
and other fish for salting, ham to smoke
in the chimney, herbs aplenty in the
gardens, and ale in the tub. It appears
there is food enough here to fill up even
the greatest of bellies."

Governor Bradford decided the English
men and women of Plymouth were most
deserving of a good English-style Harvest
Home celebration.

"Go out and tell one and all that we
must prepare for a goodly feast," he said to
Stephen Hopkins, "perhaps one that lasts
as long as three days. We will extend an
invitation to our Indian friends to join us
in the feasting."

Then he sent Edward Winslow, Isaac
Allerton, and two others "on fowling," de-
claring that they should return with "no
less than turkey, duck, and geese."

He ordered Myles Standish to take other
Pilgrim men and launch the shallop.

   "Catch a goodly amount of cod and bass
and perhaps an eel or two," he said.

The Governor told Mistress Hopkins,
Good Wife Billington, Mistress Brewster,
and Mistress Winslow that they would
prepare the food. These four were the only
married ladies to have survived "the

general sickness." They were also the only
ones skilled in the "art of cookery."

So upon his orders, the women set to
work. There was much roasting and
peeling and pounding and slicing.

Soon the village began to bustle with
activity. Desire Minter prepared the clay
oven for baking. Others kneaded loaves
of bread. Mary Allerton fetched buckets
of water. Baskets filled with herbs and
vegetables were delivered to many a
household. Wrestling Brewster chased
after chickens for slaughter and carried
more firewood than he cared to re-
member. Elizabeth Tilley and Damaris
Hopkins cooked up a huge kettle of
tasty soup, enough to feed fifty. The
Pilgrim men, meanwhile, rolled out
barrels to hold plank tops. They cov-
ered these and other tables with fine
English linen cloths.

On the day the feast began, the Indians arrived led by Massasoit, his face painted a deep red. The villagers greeted them joyfully. But much to everyone's surprise, there were ninety Indians wanting to share in the feast.

"We shall have to add more meat to the pots," Mistress Hopkins shouted to her ladies, "and put more bread to the oven."

The Indians made themselves comfortable, and Pilgrim children watched in awe while they smoked their pipes.

Smells of roasted meat, fish and fowl of every kind filled the crisp autumn air. Pilgrims and Indians alike gathered near the tables.

"You'll not find me last in line," shouted Stephen Hopkins as he ran home to fetch his trencher. "My belly is telling me 'tis time to eat."

Already in place on the tables were vessels of ale. Now bowls and trenchers laden with the very best the women could prepare were proudly brought out. The dishes included turkey with "puddings in the belly," venison, stuffed cod, goose pudding, fruit tarts, corn pasties, soup, trifle, stewed pumpkin, and salad herbs.

Everyone was more than ready to eat, so the Governor announced a time for prayer.

"Lord God Jehovah, come before us as we ask thy blessings. Thy hand has watchfully brought us to this land and given us amity with the natives that live herein. We do give solemn thanks and praises to thy name. Amen."

The eating began, and soon the children and servants were carrying food from hearth to table as fast as they could. Every so often, they snitched a morsel or gulped a drink when no one was watching. Good Wife Billington lost her spoon in the custard. And Stephen Hopkins announced, "There's naught better than eel."

The Indians smiled as they experienced new tastes and dishes.

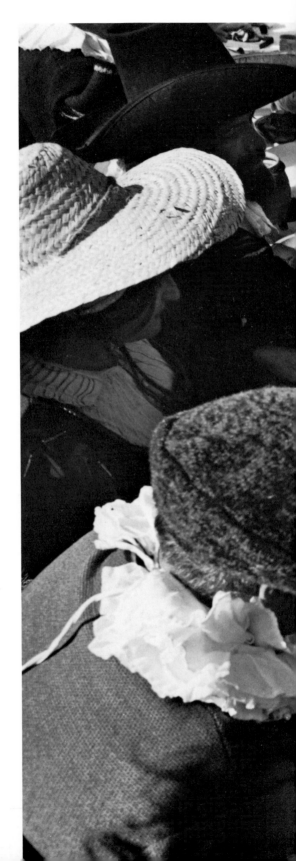

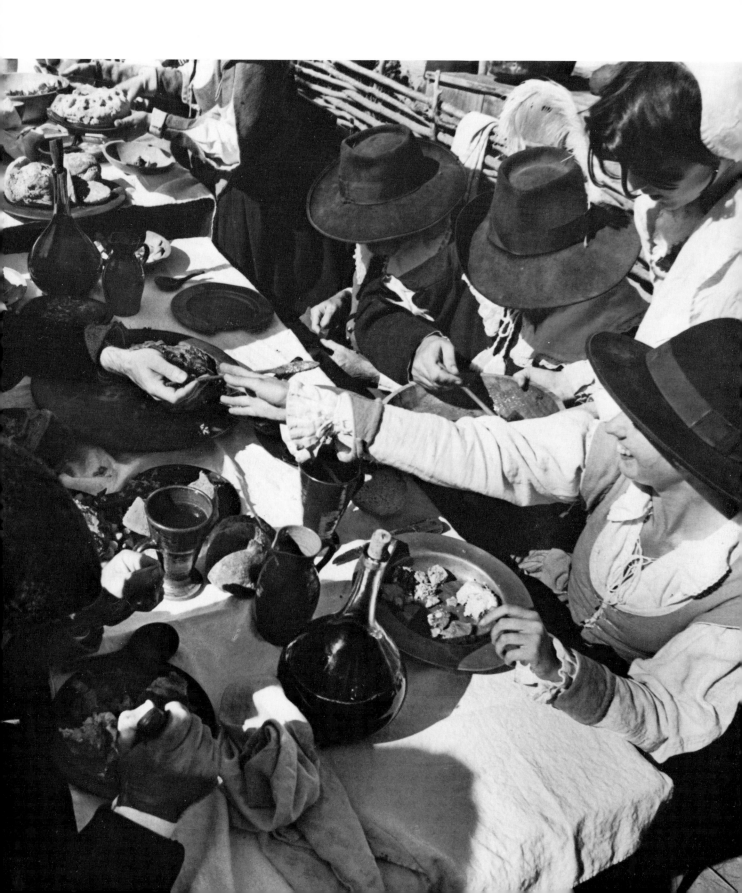

The eating went on and on and on, and when bellies were full, it was time for "general recreation."

Pillow pushing was a favorite of the children. Straddling a log, high off the

ground, two young women pounded away with pillows until one or the other fell off.

" 'Tis very good for exercising the muscles," one of the Pilgrim men shouted.

The men showed their strength pitching the bar. Each one tried to throw the huge log farther than the other.

A group of men and women engaged in a tug of war. "Come, Mistresses, try your strength," the men beckoned.

"Are ye ready?" shouted the leader. "Are ye set? Gooooooo."

There were grunts and giggles and then cheers as one side finally pulled the other over the line. It was a sight to behold, with men and women tumbling about on the ground.

One major spectacle was the "exercising of arms." Everyone followed the sounds of a drum roll to a nearby field. At Captain Standish's order, the Pilgrim men loaded their muskets, inserted the lighted wicks, and BANG! The noise, accompanied by a cloud of smoke, made "a most respectable impression" on the Indians.

Gyles Hopkins spent as much time as he could with the Indian men who spoke some English. He had never been so close to Indians before and was fascinated by their clothing and manner.

To the sound of a pipe and drum, a group of the ladies began a jigging match. Only the youngest ladies dared enter it, because the winner would be the lady who could dance to the piper the longest. "'Tis a joyful sound to hear the clapping and the breathing as one after the other drops away," Richard Warren remarked.

Then the Governor announced from the crowd that God should be remembered at that time. In response, a group of women sang the Twenty-third Psalm. Then they broke into a lovely English folk song, sung as a round.

Before long, Myles Standish shouted aloud, " 'Tis time for another dance." With much nodding of approval from the men, the women performed a formal English dance, with grace and gentility, to the strains of a lute.

The Indians watched all the activities. Then they began to plan an exhibition of their own. They formed a line behind Massasoit himself.

Singing a chant, they performed a dance full of mystery. Deer hooves jingled from their leggings. Beads of stone and bone clicked rhythmically in their necklaces.

The Pilgrims looked on in awe, while shadows began to lengthen and the afternoon grew late.

For three full days, the food kept coming and the fires burned brightly and the people of Plymouth danced and sang and frolicked and ate until they could celebrate no more. It would be years before God's blessings would be great enough to have another harvest feast as grand and joyous as this one.

The Thanksgiving Day we celebrate each November in the United States is a blend of several historical traditions. One is the New England harvest festival, and the Pilgrims' harvest feast of 1621 is a perfect example of this.

A second tradition is the religious observance of a day of prayer and thanksgiving, which sometimes included a feast. Such religious days were declared by the Pilgrims whenever they felt God had been extraordinarily good to them, no matter what the time of year. Early American presidents such as George Washington and James Monroe proclaimed similar days of thanksgiving. In 1863, President Abraham Lincoln proclaimed two such days, and one of them was the last Thursday in November. Today we celebrate our national Thanksgiving Day on the fourth Thursday in November.

There is another side to the American Thanksgiving. Some Wampanoags and other Indians gather annually on Thanksgiving Day at Plymouth Rock for a ceremony in which they declare a National Day of Mourning. These Native People believe the First Thanksgiving Feast marked the beginning of the end of their original way of life.

The Pilgrims, especially Governor William Bradford and Edward Winslow, got along well with Massasoit, Squanto, and the other Indians. But friction developed among members of later generations.

It is ironic that the very survival of the Pilgrims of Plymouth depended on Indian support. Today, the Wampanoags are asserting their cultural rights in continuing the heritage that is theirs.